GW01401402

Original title:

A Stronger Me

Author: Johan Kirsipuu

ISBN HARDBACK: 978-9916-89-730-0

ISBN PAPERBACK: 978-9916-89-731-7

ISBN EBOOK: 978-9916-89-732-4

A Heart Steeped in Faith

In shadows cast by doubt's embrace,
A whisper calls, a sacred grace.
With open hands, I raise my plea,
In every trial, there's hope to see.

The light of truth, it shines so bright,
Guiding souls through darkest night.
With every tear, a prayer is sown,
A garden bloomed in hearts unknown.

In unity, we stand as one,
Believers bound, our race is run.
With love as armor, we shall fight,
A heart steeped in faith, pure and right.

The Sanctuary of Courage

In silence deep, the spirit grows,
A fortress built where courage flows.
Beneath the weight of trials faced,
A sanctuary, love embraced.

With every step, the heart beats strong,
A melody, a sacred song.
For in the face of fears we rise,
Guided by faith, we touch the skies.

The road is long, yet light we carry,
Through storms we walk, unburdened, merry.
In hands clasped tight, the flames ignite,
The sanctuary of courage bright.

Echoes of the Celestial

In twilight's glow, the heavens sing,
A symphony of love they bring.
Stars like stories, bright and clear,
Whispers of grace that draw us near.

With every heartbeat, tune in sweet,
The dance of faith beneath our feet.
In every whisper, truth unfolds,
Echoes of the celestial, bold.

Together we find our sacred place,
With open hearts, we seek His face.
In unity, the light we share,
Echoes of the celestial, everywhere.

Rising Above the Tempest

When storms arise and shadows play,
We lift our eyes to brighter day.
With steadfast hearts, we learn to soar,
Rising above, forevermore.

Each trial faced, a lesson gained,
Through prayers spoken, doubt has waned.
In faith's embrace, our spirits meet,
Rising above, we feel complete.

As waves may crash, our truth remains,
In every heart, His love sustains.
With courage found, we claim our voice,
Rising above, we rejoice.

In the Light of Courage

In the dawn's first light, we rise,
With hearts ablaze, we reach the skies.
Where doubts fade and fears unfold,
We stand as one, courageous and bold.

With every step, our spirits soar,
Through trials faced, we seek for more.
In unity, our strength ignites,
Guided by love, we embrace the fight.

The shadows tremble in our wake,
For faith flows strong, it cannot break.
In whispers soft, the truth is clear,
In courage found, we banish fear.

When storms arise and tempests roar,
Together we shall brave the shore.
With hands entwined, we face the day,
In the light of courage, we find our way.

Transcending Shadows of Doubt

In the silence, whispers grow,
Seeds of faith we plant and sow.
Through valleys low, our spirits roam,
In shadows cast, we seek our home.

Each heartbeat sings a sacred song,
In doubt's embrace, we still belong.
With every tear, we learn to rise,
Transcending pain, we touch the skies.

The night may seem long and cold,
Yet in our hearts, a flame unfolds.
With trust restored, we walk anew,
In light divine, our vision true.

Together we rise, hand in hand,
In steadfast hope, we make our stand.
Through shadows dark, our souls take flight,
Transcending doubt, we find the light.

Blessed Rebirth

In the stillness, a whisper calls,
Through broken chains, our spirit sprawls.
In valleys deep, we find our grace,
A blessed rebirth, we embrace.

From ashes born, we rise anew,
With every dawn, our hearts break through.
In love's embrace, we shed the past,
Each moment cherished, each moment vast.

We gather strength from wounds once sore,
Hand in hand, we forge once more.
In gentle light, we learn to see,
The holy truth that sets us free.

Through trials faced, and lessons learned,
In sacred fires, our passion burned.
With every heartbeat, hope takes flight,
In blessed rebirth, we chase the light.

The Path of Unbreakable Faith

On the path where shadows lay,
We walk together, come what may.
In steadfast hearts, our visions share,
With unbreakable faith, we dare.

The stones we tread, though rough and bare,
Are stepping stones to heights so rare.
In every challenge, spirits shine,
United souls, our hearts align.

Through trials fierce and tempests bold,
Our tales of strength are yet untold.
With prayers lifted to the skies,
In grace, we rise; in love, we fly.

In every breath, a truth remains,
In faith's embrace, love breaks the chains.
Together we journey, side by side,
On paths of faith, where hope abides.

Waters of Renewal

In stillness, waters flow,
A whisper of life unseen,
Beneath the surface, hope grows,
Awakening all that's been.

From depths of silence, we rise,
Cleansed by the sacred stream,
Each drop a promise of skies,
Reflecting the Divine dream.

With every ripple, hearts mend,
Casting worries far and wide,
In the current, we transcend,
Embracing grace as our guide.

Flowing gently, the waters sing,
A hymn of love, pure and bright,
In their embrace, we take wing,
Bathed in the soft, holy light.

Stone and Spirit

Ancient stones beneath our feet,
They echo stories of the past,
Whispers of faith, strong and sweet,
Guiding us, steadfast and fast.

In every crack, a tale resides,
Of battles fought and lessons learned,
The spirit within the stone abides,
In unity, our hearts are turned.

Rich in wisdom, the earth does breathe,
A tapestry of all that's true,
From every stone, we learn to weave,
The path of love, old yet new.

Together we stand, side by side,
In strength, our spirits intertwine,
With every challenge, we abide,
Finding solace in the divine.

The Path of Stones

Upon the path of ancient stones,
Each step a prayer softly said,
Trusting the wisdom that they own,
Lighting the way as we tread.

The journey's long, yet we are one,
Guided by stars that shine bright,
Life's river flows, we follow on,
In faith, we walk into the light.

Through shadows deep, the stones remain,
Beneath our feet, a steadfast guide,
In every grain, there's love and pain,
Yet still, we rise, with hearts applied.

Together we sing in harmony,
With every challenge, we renew,
On the path, we find unity,
Knowing the love that flows is true.

Wings of Faith

Lifted high on wings of grace,
We soar above the storms that strive,
Embracing love in every place,
With faith, our spirits come alive.

Through trials faced and shadows cast,
The heart finds strength to fly and rise,
In trust, we leave the pain of past,
To spread our wings beneath the skies.

Each feather holds a prayer released,
A beacon for the weary soul,
In unity, we find our peace,
Together, we become the whole.

As burning stars ignite the night,
With wings of faith, we chase the dawn,
In love's embrace, we take our flight,
A journey blessed, forever drawn.

Rising Waters

In shadows deep, the waters rise,
A voice whispers from the skies.
Faith like a boat on turbulent seas,
Guides our hearts to calm and peace.

With every wave, a promise stands,
In His grace, we find our plans.
Storms may roar, yet we will soar,
For love abounds, forevermore.

Let not the fears overshadow night,
For dawn will break, a gentle light.
The waters bow beneath His hand,
A sacred trust we understand.

Through tempest's rage, we seek His face,
In every drop, we find His grace.
Fear not, for we are not alone,
In rising waters, love is known.

The Shield of Faithfulness

Beneath the weight of doubts and fears,
Faithfulness shines through the years.
A shield of light, it guards our hearts,
In trials faced, its strength imparts.

With every breath, we lift our song,
In unity, we all belong.
Together we stand, hand in hand,
With faith as strong as heaven's band.

When shadows creep and spirits sigh,
The shield of faith will lift us high.
In darkest hours, we will not yield,
For love protects; it is our shield.

Through battles fought, and lessons learned,
In faithful hearts, a fire burned.
We march ahead, for we are blessed,
By faithfulness, we're truly pressed.

Tides of Determination

Upon the shore, the tides will flow,
A dance of strength, the waves will show.
In hearts aflame, our spirits rise,
Determination meets the skies.

With every crest, we claim our dreams,
Like roaring tides, we bridge our seams.
Unyielding hearts, together we'll stand,
In storms of life, we hold His hand.

Each challenge met, we grow more strong,
With faith as our guide, we belong.
The tides of time may shift and sway,
But with resolve, we'll find our way.

The ocean vast, it calls our name,
To rise and shine, to stake our claim.
With every wave, the spirit wakes,
Determination in our wakes.

The Lantern of Resolve

In the hush of night, a lantern glows,
Its gentle light leads where hope flows.
A beacon bright in trials faced,
With every step, His love embraced.

Through shadows deep, we find our path,
The lantern shines, dispelling wrath.
With courage bold and eyes alight,
We walk in faith, dispelling night.

Each flicker speaks of dreams anew,
The lantern guides us, pure and true.
In moments dim, it shines our way,
With love's embrace, we will not stray.

A symbol strong, our hearts entwined,
In every heartbeat, love defined.
The lantern's glow, forever near,
In resolve, we cast aside our fear.

Walk of Valor

In shadows deep, we tread the path,
With faith as light, and love our wrath.
Through trials fierce, with hearts aglow,
We rise, we stand, we walk the flow.

Each step we take, a prayer we weave,
In armor strong, we dare believe.
The courage born from sacred trust,
A pledge to rise from sacred dust.

Through storms that rage and flames that burn,
We seek the peace that we shall earn.
With valor bright, we face the night,
Forever bound in holy sight.

The call of faith, our hearts embrace,
In trials faced, we find our grace.
In every trial, a lesson streams,
In walk of valor, we fulfill dreams.

In the Wake of Turmoil

When chaos whispers, we seek the calm,
In sacred trust, we find our balm.
Amidst the storm, we lift our prayer,
A beacon bright, in wide despair.

In shadows cast, where doubts reside,
We turn to Him, our faithful guide.
In wake of anguish, hope shall rise,
As light divine breaks through the skies.

With every tear, a seed we sow,
In fields of pain, love's rivers flow.
Through strife we learn, in trials steep,
Our hearts will bloom, our souls will leap.

The path is rough, yet we shall forge,
Through nights of struggle, we urge and urge.
In faith's embrace, we find our way,
In wake of turmoil, we choose to pray.

Anchored in Belief

In tempest's roar, we set our sail,
With hope our anchor, we shall not fail.
Through waters fierce, we chart our course,
In faith alone, we find our force.

When doubts arise, we lift our gaze,
To skies above, in light we blaze.
Anchored firm, our spirits soar,
In love bestowed, we seek no more.

With every wave that crashes down,
We wear our faith like royal crown.
Through every storm, we hold it tight,
In depths of night, we seek the light.

With hearts united, we shall prevail,
In trials faced, we will tell the tale.
Anchored in belief, we find our peace,
In grace divine, our doubts release.

Harvest of Trials

In fields of sorrow, we sow our tears,
With faith as soil, we grow through fears.
In trials hard, we plant our dreams,
With every struggle, hope redeems.

The harvest comes from seeds of pain,
In darkest nights, we shall remain.
The fruit of labor, ripe and sweet,
With love's embrace, we claim our seat.

Through every doubt, a lesson blooms,
In trials faced, the spirit looms.
From barren grounds, we rise anew,
The harvest of trials, pure and true.

As dawn breaks forth, we stand in awe,
The blessings found in every flaw.
In every tear, a joy concealed,
In faith we trust, our hearts revealed.

The Bridge Over Stormy Waters

In trials fierce and waters deep,
We seek the light, our souls to keep.
A bridge of hope spans wide and far,
Guiding us to where You are.

Through raging storms, Your hand we grasp,
In every struggle, we find our clasp.
With faith our compass, peace our sail,
Together we shall never fail.

The raging seas may rise and swell,
Yet through the tempest, all is well.
On holy ground, our hearts align,
In every storm, Your love's design.

You calm the waves, make silence fall,
With whispered grace, You hear our call.
A bridge of mercy, strong and true,
Our hearts, dear Lord, will rest in You.

The Soul's Resounding Echo

Within the silence, whispers sing,
The echoes of our souls take wing.
In quietude, truths gently unfold,
With every heartbeat, tales retold.

Your voice, O Lord, a guiding light,
Illuminates the darkest night.
Each echo carries blessings near,
In every shadow, love draws near.

As mountains tremble, and heavens sway,
Your presence beckons, come what may.
The depths of sorrow cannot hold,
In Your embrace, we turn to gold.

Awake our souls to realms above,
In harmony, we share Your love.
The echoes blend, a sacred sound,
In unity, our lives abound.

Firm Foundations in the Spirit

Upon the rock, we build our faith,
In trials fierce, our hearts won't wraith.
A foundation, strong and deep,
In every promise, You shall keep.

With nails of truth and beams of grace,
We raise our hearts in holy space.
The spirit guides with every breath,
In life's embrace, we conquer death.

Your love, a mortar hard and true,
In every challenge, we lean on You.
With courage firm, our spirits soar,
In standing tall, we seek You more.

In unity of heart and mind,
With faith unyielding, love aligned.
Our firm foundations will not shake,
In every promise that You make.

When Faith Meets Fortitude

In moments dark, where shadows loom,
Our faith ignites, dispelling gloom.
With fortitude, we rise anew,
In every challenge, we find You.

The mountain's peak may seem afar,
Yet faith will guide, our shining star.
With every step, we're not alone,
In strength, O Lord, Your love is shown.

Through trials faced, our spirits bloom,
In depths of night, love breaks the gloom.
With hearts aflame, we stand our ground,
In faith and fortitude, we're found.

Together, Lord, we journey on,
In every dawn, a brand new song.
When faith and fortitude combine,
In this embrace, our hopes align.

The Song of the Unyielding

In shadows deep, we stand our ground,
With voices raised, our faith resounds.
Through storms that rage, we hold the flame,
In trials faced, we call His name.

The heart of stone, now soft and warm,
In every wound, His love transforms.
A song of hope, we sing as one,
In unity, the battle's won.

With lifted hands, we seek His face,
In every struggle, find His grace.
The path ahead may twist and bend,
But with His strength, we shall ascend.

The stars above, a guiding light,
In darkest hours, they shine so bright.
No fear shall claim, no doubt intrude,
For in His arms, we are renewed.

Our spirits soar, like eagles high,
Where faith abounds, our souls comply.
In every note, our hearts align,
In steadfast love, His will, divine.

Through the Valley of Trials

In the valley where shadows dwell,
Each step we take, we know too well.
With faith as our shield, we move forth brave,
In every trial, find strength to save.

The road is rough, the journey long,
Yet in our hearts, we sing a song.
With hope as our light, we press on near,
In darkest nights, His voice we hear.

Through whispers soft, and winds that howl,
Our souls awakened, we will not cowl.
For in the depths, His grace we find,
A promise sealed, with love entwined.

The river flows, through tough terrain,
Where tears may fall, we rise again.
In every wound, His mercy poured,
Through valleys low, we find the Lord.

With every step, we gather strength,
Together we walk, no fear at length.
In trials faced, we learn to stand,
For in His care, our lives are planned.

A Heart Forged in Faith

In quiet moments, we seek the truth,
A heart ignited, restored in youth.
With every prayer, our spirits soar,
A love unwavering, we will explore.

Through challenges faced, we rise anew,
In each abode, a guiding view.
With joy in trials, our souls refine,
In Him alone, our hearts entwine.

The darkness fades, the dawn breaks bright,
In every struggle, find the light.
Forged in faith, our purpose clear,
With every heartbeat, we draw Him near.

In moments fierce, His peace we cherish,
From pain arises, love won't perish.
With steadfast courage, our voices cry,
In all we face, with Him we fly.

With arms wide open, we welcome grace,
In every heartbeat, His love we trace.
A heart reborn, from ashes rise,
In faith we trust, our spirits ties.

The Light Beyond Despair

In the depths where shadows creep,
A flicker stirs, our souls to keep.
With every tear, a whisper calls,
In darkest nights, His love befalls.

Through trials faced, we seek the dawn,
A light ignited, hope reborn.
With each step forward, fear must flee,
For in His grace, we are set free.

The path may twist, and hills may rise,
Yet in our hearts, His truth never lies.
With heavy burdens, we journey on,
Through storms we weather, our faith is strong.

In every moment, His peace we claim,
Through sullen nights, we praise His name.
For in despair, joy intertwines,
A quilt of grace, our hearts it binds.

With open arms, we embrace the light,
For in our pain, He shines so bright.
Together we stand, unbroken and sure,
In the light beyond, our hearts endure.

Sculpted by Adversity

In trials we find our strength anew,
Each wound a lesson, each scar a clue.
The hands of fate shape our weary souls,
Molding our hearts to embrace greater goals.

In storms, our spirits begin to rise,
A fiery forge beneath darkened skies.
Through shadows of doubt, we stand our ground,
In faith we stumble, yet love is found.

Each challenge faced, a step toward grace,
The burdens we carry with humble pace.
From ashes we spring, reborn, refined,
A testament to the strength of the mind.

Like clay in the hands of the potter's art,
We yearn for the flame that ignites the heart.
Embracing the struggle, we find our way,
In blessings hidden, life's bright array.

The Promise of Renewal

In the darkness, hope shines so bright,
Whispers of dawn, a softening light.
The seed must break for the bloom to start,
In shadows we learn, in silence, the heart.

From whispers of winter, springs forth the song,
Each note a promise, where we belong.
Through trials we travel, with faith as our guide,
The rivers of sorrow will turn with the tide.

The earth awakens, as do our dreams,
In color and fragrance, the spirit redeems.
With every heartbeat, new life we find,
In echoes of love that will never unwind.

A tapestry woven with threads of grace,
In each wounded moment, the hope we embrace.
For every ending, a beginning anew,
The promise of renewal shines ever true.

Songs of the Forged Spirit

Within the forge where our spirits bend,
We are molded by fire, with truths to defend.
Each blow of the hammer, a note in the song,
A melody fierce, where we all belong.

Our voices unite in the battle of life,
Through peace and through chaos, through joy and
through strife.
A choir of hearts, each note standing tall,
In the symphony crafted, we answer the call.

Resilience flows in our veins like a stream,
Through struggles we gather, in unity dream.
For every challenge that bends our will,
A chorus of courage sings louder still.

The fires of passion, ignited and bright,
Our spirits ascend in the dark of the night.
Together we rise, a testament bold,
In songs of the forged spirit, our stories unfold.

Rooted in Love

In gardens of grace, our roots intertwine,
A tapestry woven, our hearts align.
From soil to sky, our dreams take flight,
In the warmth of love, we illuminate the night.

Each moment we share, a seed that we sow,
Nurtured in patience, through ebb and flow.
With each gentle whisper, a promise we make,
Together we stand, in the love we create.

Through trials and triumphs, hand in hand we grow,
In the bonds of devotion, the light starts to glow.
For love is our anchor, steadfast and true,
In the garden of life, forever renewed.

Let storms come and go, we will not be swayed,
For love is our shelter, where hope is displayed.
In every embrace, we find strength above,
For we are not lost, we are rooted in love.

Rising from the Ashes

In shadows deep, I find my grace,
A whisper soft, a warm embrace.
From ashes cold, my spirit lifts,
Renewed in hope, the heart it sifts.

Through trials fierce, the flames do rise,
Yet through the smoke, I see the skies.
A phoenix born from pain's embrace,
In every struggle, I find my place.

The scars I bear, a sacred mark,
A journey bright, igniting spark.
With every step, the past I free,
In faith's bright light, I rise to be.

The heart once broken learns to mend,
In love's true arms, I find my friend.
Awake, arise, no fear to show,
For from the ashes, I shall grow.

With strength renewed, I walk my path,
The joy I seek transcends the wrath.
In every tear, a lesson shines,
From ashes cold, my spirit climbs.

The Fortress Within

Deep in my soul, a fortress stands,
Built on the rock of faith-filled hands.
Though storms may rage, my heart is still,
Anchored firm by God's own will.

With walls of strength and towers high,
I find my peace; I will not cry.
In every challenge, I stand tall,
For in His love, I'll never fall.

The whispers doubt may try to break,
Yet in His promise, I awake.
Resilience grows from every stone,
In silence deep, I've found my own.

The light within, a guiding flame,
Draws me to seek His holy name.
In battles won and battles lost,
I build my faith regardless of cost.

With faith as armor, I press on,
A warrior's heart from dusk till dawn.
This fortress stands, my shield, my kin,
A heavenly peace, the worth of win.

Grace in Trials

In darkest nights, His light does gleam,
A gentle touch, a flowing stream.
Through trials fierce, His love remains,
In every heartache, hope sustains.

Each tear I shed, a prayer I send,
In every struggle, He's my friend.
With grace bestowed in times of strife,
He walks beside me, gives me life.

Though paths may twist and shadows loom,
His whispered words dispel the gloom.
In every trial, wisdom grows,
Through every test, His mercy flows.

The challenges I face each day,
Transform my heart, in Him I sway.
For in the storm, I feel Him near,
His grace, my anchor, calms my fear.

With every dawn, a chance to rise,
To find the strength in borrowed skies.
In trials faced, I learn to see,
The grace divine that lives in me.

Cloaked in Resilience

Wrapped in courage, my spirit glows,
In trials faced, my faith still grows.
Cloaked in strength, the burdens fall,
With every rise, I heed the call.

The storms may howl, the darkness creep,
Yet in my heart, the light will seep.
Resilience swells like ocean tide,
In every challenge, I will abide.

With every bruise, I wear my soul,
In brokenness, I find the whole.
As thorns may press, I stand my ground,
In silent strength, my peace is found.

The fabric woven with threads of grace,
In trials faced, I find my place.
Each step I take on rocky soil,
Stands testament to strength in toil.

For in this journey, love will bind,
Emerging whole, I seek to find.
Cloaked in resilience, I rise and sing,
For in my heart, His praises ring.

Rise Up in Grace

In the shadows we find light,
Guiding hearts through the night.
With each whisper of prayer,
Sinners rise in purest care.

Cast aside all earthly fears,
With faith flowing like bright tears.
Lift your hands, embrace the sky,
For in grace, we learn to fly.

Mountains tremble at His name,
Burning bright, eternal flame.
Stand as one, united strong,
In His love, we all belong.

Through the valleys, on we tread,
With His promise, never dread.
Rise again, and do not break,
In His mercy, souls awake.

Hearts of stone to flesh renewed,
In His arms, all pain subdued.
Rise up now, embrace the call,
In His grace, we shall not fall.

Unyielding Spirit of Hope

Words of wisdom softly sung,
In the silence, hearts are strung.
Hope's foundation, firm and free,
Guides us to our destiny.

In the tempest, stand your ground,
With a faith that knows no bound.
Every trial, a stepping stone,
In our struggle, we have grown.

Through the darkness, still we rise,
With the love that never dies.
Each new day, a gift to see,
In His presence, we are free.

Lift your eyes, the dawn is near,
With each heartbeat, shed the fear.
Trust in grace, let burdens go,
In His arms, our spirits grow.

With each wound, a chance to mend,
Unyielding hope, our truest friend.
Forward ever, never back,
In His light, we stay on track.

Radiance Through Trials

In the fire, gold is found,
Searing pain, the truth unbound.
With each struggle, strength is born,
As we rise with each new dawn.

Though the journey winds and bends,
Every heartache gently tends.
Flee the shadows, step to light,
Radiance breaks the darkest night.

Faith like mountains, strong and sure,
In His love, our souls endure.
Joy arises from the sorrow,
Guiding us to a new tomorrow.

When despair looms overhead,
Trust the path where angels tread.
In the storm, we find our way,
With each moment, learn to pray.

Grace encircles every fight,
Through the trials, find the light.
Radiant hearts shall never dim,
In His grace, we rise again.

The Alchemy of Endurance

From the ashes, new life springs,
In our hearts, His glory sings.
Through the struggle, learn to grow,
In endurance, love will flow.

Transform pain to pureness bright,
As we journey toward the light.
Hope ignites the weary soul,
In His hands, we become whole.

Hold the thread of faith so tight,
Weaving dreams in darkest night.
With each step, we learn to bend,
From the start until the end.

With each challenge, wisdom gained,
Through our losses, hearts unchained.
In His presence, find your grace,
Through the trials, seek His face.

Let the winds of change embrace,
Through the storm, we learn our place.
The alchemy, divine and true,
In endurance, life renews.

The Banner of Belief

Raise high the flag of faith,
In each heart it shall dwell,
Through storms and trials,
We hold onto the swell.

In unity we gather,
With voices pure and clear,
A chorus of love's power,
Each echo draws us near.

The banner waves in grace,
A symbol of our trust,
With every step we take,
In Him, we find our thrust.

We march on paths unknown,
Encouragement from above,
With every prayer we sew,
Together, bound by love.

So let us rise as one,
With hope as our embrace,
Beneath the shining sun,
We carry His great grace.

The Armor of Grace

In the morning's gentle light,
We don the armor bright,
With kindness as our shield,
And love our guiding sight.

Each piece a sacred gift,
To guard against the night,
Against sorrow's heavy toll,
We stand prepared to fight.

With faith to forge our sword,
Our hearts are set aflame,
With every blow of doubt,
We strengthen love's great name.

The shoes of peace we wear,
Upon this blessed ground,
With every stride we take,
Our joy is surely found.

So let us band together,
With grace as our embrace,
In every challenge faced,
We wear the armor of grace.

Climbing the Mountain of Trials

With every step I climb,
The summit calls my name,
Though rocks may bruise my feet,
My spirit fuels the flame.

The path is steep and winding,
Yet faith is my trail guide,
Each struggle hones my strength,
With love, I shall abide.

Through fog of doubt and fear,
I reach for heavenly light,
With hope in every breath,
I conquer darkest night.

The mountain's peak, a promise,
Of peace that waits above,
With every prayer I whisper,
I climb on wings of love.

So onward in my journey,
I find the will to rise,
For each trial leads me closer,
To the light of heaven's skies.

From Shadows to the Sunlit Path

In shadows deep and cold,
A whisper calls my name,
With every tear I've shed,
I rise, and not in vain.

The dawn begins to break,
With colors warm and bright,
Each ray a sacred promise,
Driven by love's pure light.

I leave the past behind,
Embracing what's ahead,
With faith as my compass,
In Christ, I am well-fed.

The path of life unfolds,
With every step I take,
Through valleys of the lost,
It's love that guides my wake.

From shadows into day,
I walk with hope anew,
In every heart's embrace,
The sun is shining through.

The Hidden Warrior

In shadows deep, the faithful tread,
With hearts of courage, unafraid.
They lift the weak, with strength anew,
A hidden warrior, tried and true.

Through storms of doubt and trials fierce,
Their spirits strong, they do not pierce.
A mighty force, though seldom seen,
In silent prayers, their hopes convene.

With armor made of love and grace,
They stand with faith, a steady pace.
For every battle fought in night,
Their souls emerge, anointed light.

In whispers soft, the angels guide,
The hidden warrior, standing pride.
They forge ahead, where few have trod,
With every step, they honor God.

And when the dawn breaks through the sky,
The hidden warrior will not die.
For in their heart, a fire burns bright,
A testament to love and light.

Sacred Seeds of Hope

In barren fields where shadows creep,
A seed of hope begins to leap.
With care and prayer, it finds the ground,
In sacred soil, new life is found.

Each drop of rain, each ray of sun,
Nurtures the dreams, each battle won.
Through trials fierce, the roots grow strong,
In silent faith, they hum their song.

The winds may howl, the storms may rage,
Yet hope endures, a golden page.
Each blossom bright, a lesson learned,
Sacred seeds of hope, forever yearned.

With every bloom, a story shared,
Of love's embrace, a life declared.
In hearts awakened, joy will swell,
For sacred seeds, their tales compel.

And when the harvest finally comes,
The faithful dance, the joyous drums.
In gratitude, their voices rise,
For sacred seeds beneath the skies.

Illuminated by Trials

Through trials deep, our spirits soar,
We learn to open every door.
In darkest nights, a light will gleam,
A guiding star, a cherished dream.

Each test we face, a chance to grow,
With every wound, new wisdom flows.
Illuminated paths unfold,
Our stories rich, our hearts bold.

In unity, we rise as one,
With prayers lifted, battles won.
For strength is found in arms embraced,
In trials faced, our fears erased.

With every step, we find our way,
Through storms of doubt and skies of gray.
Illuminated by faith's embrace,
We walk together, seeking grace.

And when the dawn breaks sweet and clear,
We lift our voices, banish fear.
For every trial, a step we climb,
In love's embrace, we intertwine.

From Brokenness to Restoration

In shattered pieces, hope resides,
A fragile heart, through pain it hides.
Yet in the cracks, a light breaks through,
From brokenness, we begin anew.

With every tear, a prayer ascends,
In darkest nights, the soul extends.
Restoration waits, a promise clear,
In grace's arms, we cast out fear.

The potter's hand, so skilled and wise,
Reforms our hearts, a sweet surprise.
From ashes rise, we see the dawn,
From brokenness, a hope reborn.

We gather strength from every fall,
In unity, we heed the call.
For every wound, a tale retold,
In restoration, our hearts unfold.

And when we stand, renewed and free,
We rise in love, in harmony.
From brokenness, we find our way,
To brighter paths, a new display.

The Fortress of Belief

In the shadows where doubt may dwell,
Faith stands sturdy, a timeless shell.
With every whisper of the night,
The heart is anchored, held in light.

Through trials faced, we find our ground,
In prayer's embrace, our peace is found.
Guarded by love, we rise and soar,
In the fortress, we are evermore.

The walls of trust, built strong and high,
Shields against the tears that cry.
Hopeful visions guide our sight,
Through darkest valleys, into light.

With each step forged on hallowed ground,
We gather strength in love profound.
Beneath the skies, we lift our voice,
In unity, we make our choice.

The fortress of belief stands tall,
A sanctuary that will not fall.
In every heart, its echoes dwell,
A sacred truth we know so well.

The Journey to Inner Glory

With every dawn, a path unfolds,
Guided by light, as the story unfolds.
Steps of faith lead to the divine,
In silence, we find the sacred sign.

Mountains high, valleys low,
In the heart's quest, true love will grow.
The soul ascends through pain and grace,
Finding purpose in every place.

Winds of change may whisper fears,
Yet hope ignites, and wipes the tears.
Each lesson learned, a jewel bright,
A guiding star in the darkest night.

In the tapestry of life, we weave,
Threads of mercy, our hearts believe.
A journey deeper, towards the light,
Transforming shadows into sight.

With every heartbeat, we draw near,
The glory whispered, loud and clear.
The journey leads where love does shine,
In unity, our souls align.

Reclaimed by Grace

In the stillness, a voice calls near,
Whispers of love, calming fear.
From brokenness, we rise anew,
In arms of grace, the heart breaks through.

Past burdens lift, like leaves in flight,
Embraced by mercy, shining bright.
The chains of doubt fall to the ground,
In unity, our spirits are found.

Through trials faced, we find our way,
With faith as lantern, day by day.
Each step we take, reclaimed in peace,
In every heart, our wounds release.

A gentle hand, a guiding light,
In every shadow, love ignites.
Reclaimed by grace, our spirits soar,
Together, stronger than before.

In the journey's tale, we stand as one,
Beneath the stars, the healing's begun.
With every moment, a chance to mend,
In grace, our stories beautifully blend.

Fountains of Hope

Amidst the parched earth, springs arise,
Fountains of hope beneath the skies.
With every drop, a promise rains,
Quenching thirst where love sustains.

In barren landscapes, flowers bloom,
Life's sweet fragrance dispels the gloom.
The heart finds melody in the strife,
In honor of resilience, the song of life.

Streams of kindness flow from within,
Washing away the weight of sin.
With open arms, we share our grace,
Creating beauty in every space.

In unity, we thirst for peace,
A fountain's blessing that will not cease.
From troubled waters, we shall rise,
Reflecting love in every guise.

Fountains of hope, forever flow,
With every heartbeat, let love grow.
In the light of faith, together we cope,
In every soul, the pulse of hope.

Embraced by His Love

In shadows deep, His love does glow,
A gentle touch that soothes our soul.
With open arms, He draws us near,
In every prayer, we quell our fear.

His mercy rains like softest dew,
Forgiveness blooms in hearts anew.
Each whispered grace, a sacred song,
In Him, we find where we belong.

Through trials fierce, His light remains,
A steady hand that breaks our chains.
Embraced by love, we stand so tall,
In faith we rise, we will not fall.

The path may twist in dark of night,
But in His warmth, we find our light.
With every step, He guides our way,
His love, our shield, come what may.

Forever wrapped in mercy's grace,
We journey on through time and space.
Embraced by Him, we come alive,
In His embrace, our spirits thrive.

Soaring on Wings of Faith

Upon the winds of hope we soar,
With hearts aflame, we seek Him more.
Each prayer a lift, each hymn a flight,
In faith we rise, embracing light.

The mountains high, the valleys low,
In every storm, His love will flow.
We spread our wings, we trust His plan,
With every heartbeat, we take a stand.

From trials faced, our spirits grow,
In darkest hours, His presence glows.
The skies may change, but we remain,
Soaring above, despite the pain.

Each step we take, in grace we move,
With every breath, His life we prove.
In unity, our hearts align,
Soaring on faith, His love divine.

Together we rise, hand in hand,
A faithful flock across this land.
Soaring on wings of faith and grace,
In God's embrace, we find our place.

The Ladder to Divine Resilience

With every rung, we climb so high,
Through trials and tears, beneath the sky.
The ladder stands, a gift from Him,
In faith we rise, where hope won't dim.

Each step we take, a lesson learned,
In flames of strife, our hearts have burned.
He strengthens us through every fall,
The ladder leads, we hear His call.

From humble roots, our spirits bloom,
In darkest nights, we push through gloom.
With every heartbeat, we ascend,
The journey long, but He's our friend.

Through struggles faced, our souls refine,
Each challenge met, His love divine.
Resilience grows in every trial,
The ladder leads us, step by mile.

In unity, we climb as one,
Our battles fought, our race not run.
The ladder strong, our spirits rise,
In faith we reach for heaven's skies.

Guided by Inner Light

In silent whispers, truth awakes,
Guided by light, our spirit shakes.
With every dawn, a chance to see,
His inner glow, illuminating me.

Through shadows cast, His love will shine,
With faithful hearts, our paths align.
A beacon bright through darkest night,
In every moment, seek the light.

With open eyes, we find our way,
In sacred grace, we choose to stay.
His light within, a guiding star,
In every breath, we know who we are.

Together we walk, hand in hand,
In perfect peace, we understand.
With hearts aglow, we rise above,
Guided by light, surrounded by love.

Embraced by grace, our spirits soar,
With every heartbeat, we seek for more.
In unity, we shine so bright,
Forever guided by inner light.

Crown of Thorns and Glory

Upon the brow a burden lies,
A crown of thorns, yet lifts us high.
Through pain and strife, we find our way,
To glory's light, we toil and pray.

The path is steep, the journey long,
Yet hearts united bloom in song.
In sacrifice, true love will show,
The seeds we plant in faith will grow.

With every tear, a lesson learned,
In darkest hours, our spirits burned.
We rise anew, with grace we stand,
Transformed by love, a gentle hand.

The thorns may pierce, the doubts may wane,
But in our hearts, we bear no blame.
For who can touch what faith has sown?
In thorns we find the truest throne.

So let us wear these crowns with pride,
In every thorn, our Spirit's guide.
For from the pain, our joy will spring,
In thorns and glory, we take wing.

Embracing the Light

In the silence of the night,
We seek the dawn, we chase the light.
With humble hearts, we raise our prayers,
In every breath, His love declares.

The shadows fade, the darkness clears,
As faith ignites, dispelling fears.
With open arms, we greet the day,
In radiant hope, we find our way.

Each step we take, a sacred vow,
To honor Him, in here and now.
For in His warmth, our souls unite,
Together strong, embracing light.

Through trials faced, we learn to trust,
In every moment, love is just.
With every smile, we share the grace,
A heavenly touch in every place.

As morning breaks, our spirits soar,
In every heart, He opens doors.
With every heartbeat, love will guide,
For in His light, we shall abide.

Echoes of Hope

In whispers soft, hope sings its tune,
Through darkest nights and blazing noon.
With each new dawn, we rise anew,
In every heart, dreams break through.

The trials faced, a test of faith,
Yet in our souls, we find our strength.
With courage firm, we stand as one,
In hope's embrace, we find the sun.

For every tear, a river flows,
In love's embrace, our spirit grows.
With every challenge, we stand tall,
In echoes of hope, we won't fall.

As storms may rage, yet still we sing,
A melody of hope takes wing.
In unity, our voices rise,
Together strong, beneath the skies.

So let us carry hope's sweet call,
In every heart, it conquers all.
With faith as guide, our spirits cope,
In every echo, we embrace hope.

From Shadows to Radiance

In shadows cast, we seek the spark,
A glimmer bright within the dark.
With faith as lantern, we move forth,
In search of joy, to claim our worth.

Through valleys low, and mountains high,
We tread with trust, with heads held high.
For in the depths, our spirits grow,
From shadows deep, to light we go.

As dawn breaks clear, we lift our praise,
In every moment, love's embrace.
With open hearts, we shine so bright,
From shadows past, we find our light.

The journey taught, with grace we'll rise,
Through every trial, the soul complies.
In unity, we glow and gleam,
For in our hearts, we chase the dream.

So let us walk, in faith's embrace,
With every step, we run the race.
From shadows dim, our spirits dance,
In radiance found, we take our stance.

Threads of Divine Perseverance

In shadows cast by doubt and fear,
We hold the threads that draw us near.
With hands entwined in prayer's embrace,
We rise anew, we find our place.

Each strand a sign of love's design,
A tapestry that intertwines.
With every struggle, hope remains,
In holy whispers, grace sustains.

Through trials faced and burdens borne,
A strength is forged, from faith reborn.
The golden threads of trust and light,
We weave our dreams in sacred sight.

Stars guide our path through darkest nights,
Our spirits soar in soaring flights.
With every heartbeat, we proclaim,
The threads of faith will never wane.

The Strength Within the Silence

In quietude, the spirit gleams,
A solace found in whispered dreams.
The weight of words can fade away,
In silence, truth begins to sway.

Amidst the noise, we learn to see,
The strength within humility.
With faith as anchor, hearts align,
In stillness, grace feels so divine.

A language spoken without sound,
In every pause, a love profound.
Here lies the courage to embrace,
Each moment wrapped in warmest grace.

The silence speaks the loudest hymn,
Exalting hearts when hope seems dim.
With every thought that's left unvoiced,
We find the strength in love's rejoiced.

Armor of the Faithful

With shields of hope and swords of grace,
We walk the path to seek His face.
In every battle, trust will guide,
The faithful's heart, our truest pride.

Each piece of armor, love adorned,
Our spirits soar, in courage born.
With faith as shield, we stand as one,
In darkest hours, we'll find the sun.

The morning light will break and shine,
Upon the souls who stand in line.
With hands held high, we rise as strong,
Together in this sacred song.

Through trials faced and fears confessed,
In faith we stand, forever blessed.
The armor worn with purpose true,
Our hearts united, ever new.

The Resurrected Heart

In shadows deep, where hope concealed,
The heart awakens, love revealed.
From ashes risen, pure and bright,
A flicker sparks, igniting light.

The journey long, through pain and loss,
Yet, in the depth, we find our cross.
A heart transformed through every tear,
In grace, we find a Savior near.

With every beat, the promise stays,
Eternal joy through darkest days.
The resurrections of the soul,
In love, we find our precious goal.

Each story told, a testament,
Of lives renewed, and hearts unbent.
In every prayer, our spirits soar,
The resurrected heart, restored.

Embracing Sacred Struggles

In shadows deep, we find our way,
Through trials fierce, we learn to pray.
Each wound a lesson, each tear a gift,
In sacred struggles, our spirits lift.

With faith as our anchor, we rise once more,
In the heart's tempest, we walk ashore.
The path may be rocky, yet grace guides us,
Transforming burden into holy trust.

As thorns may prick, the roses bloom,
In darkest nights, we shun the gloom.
Together we gather, hands intertwined,
In unity's strength, our souls aligned.

Each step a journey, each moment a chance,
In faith's embrace, we learn to dance.
For every struggle shapes our light,
Into the day that follows night.

So here we stand, unyielding and bold,
Our hearts aflame with stories untold.
Embracing the toil, we find our song,
In sacred struggles, where we belong.

The Depths of Divine Resolve

In stillness deep, the Spirit calls,
Through trials and fears, our faith enthralls.
With every doubt, the heart grows strong,
In divine resolve, we find our song.

The mountain's shadow may loom above,
Yet in our hearts, we hold His love.
Each struggle faced, a testament clear,
In the depths of grace, we conquer fear.

With whispered prayers, we seek the way,
Guided by light, we choose to stay.
For in the fight, true purpose shines,
In divine resolve, our spirit aligns.

Through tears and trials, we rise anew,
In faith's embrace, our strength we grew.
The depths we traverse shape our core,
In divine unison, we soar and explore.

With hearts ablaze and spirits free,
In unity's song, we're meant to be.
The path may twist, but hope prevails,
In the depths of divine, our resolve sails.

The Dance of Endurance

With every heartbeat, the rhythm plays,
In trials faced, we learn to praise.
In the dance of life, we sway and twirl,
Each step a blessing, both fierce and pearl.

Through tempest's roar and silence deep,
With grace as our guide, our faith we keep.
In every stumble, we find our way,
The dance of endurance, come what may.

With hands raised high, we lift our song,
In unity's embrace, we all belong.
Through weary nights and dawn so bright,
In the dance of hope, we find our light.

Each challenge faced is a step we take,
In rhythm with grace, no fear to break.
For in this dance, we find our might,
With love as our lead, we take to flight.

As flows the music, our hearts unite,
In the dance of endurance, we feel the height.
Together we flourish, against the tide,
In the sacred rhythm, where love abides.

The Flow of Heavenly Support

In whispers soft, the heavens hear,
Our prayers ascend, erasing fear.
In every moment, we're not alone,
In heavenly support, the love is shown.

Through valleys low and mountains high,
With faith as wings, we learn to fly.
In tender grace, our burdens shared,
In the flow of hope, our hearts prepared.

As storms may rage, the calm will come,
Wherever we wander, we find our home.
Each hand that reaches becomes a bridge,
In the divine flow, we cross each ridge.

With love's embrace, we stand as one,
In harmony's light, our spirits run.
When shadows fall, the stars will glow,
In heavenly support, we learn to grow.

So let us share our dreams and fears,
In the flow of grace, dissolve the tears.
For together we rise, united and free,
In the boundless flow of harmony.

The Garden of Resilience

In the quiet dawn, hope's light will shine,
Roots grow deep in faith's design.
We weather storms, we face the night,
Nurtured by love, we rise in might.

Each seed we plant, a prayer in the earth,
Strength blooms, revealing its worth.
With every tear, a river flows,
In the garden of grace, our spirit grows.

The sun will set, yet stars appear,
Guiding our path, casting out fear.
In sacred soil, our dreams take flight,
Embracing the dark, we seek the light.

Hand in hand, we sing our song,
In the heart of the garden, we all belong.
Through trials faced and burdens shared,
Together we stand, together we dared.

The seasons change, yet we remain,
In unity's strength, we break each chain.
Our roots entwined, an unbreakable bond,
In the garden of resilience, forever we're fond.

Anchored in the Spirit

In the depths of silence, a whisper calls,
Silent prayers rise, as darkness falls.
With every heartbeat, we find our way,
Anchored in Spirit, come what may.

The waves may crash and winds may roar,
Our faith, a compass, guiding ashore.
Through shadows cast and trials we face,
Embracing the journey, we find our grace.

In moments lost, when we may stray,
The light of the Spirit shows us the way.
Each step forward, a sacred vow,
Grounded in truth, we prosper now.

With hearts united, we rise as one,
In the glow of the Spirit, battles are won.
Through storms we sail, with hope as our sail,
In the depths of the soul, our faith will prevail.

Together we seek, together we roam,
Anchored in love, we always find home.
With every tide, we fiercely uphold,
In the arms of the Spirit, our stories unfold.

Wings of the Divine

In the stillness of night, whispers take flight,
Carried by angels, wrapped in light.
On wings of the Divine, we soar above,
Guided by peace, embraced by love.

The heavens open, revealing the way,
With every moment, we're blessed each day.
In trials and triumphs, we find the grace,
With wings of the Divine, we find our place.

The clouds may gather, the tempest may rage,
Yet faith will lift us from stage to stage.
In the arms of the sky, our spirits intertwine,
Together we rise, on wings of the Divine.

From heights we gather, wisdom and peace,
In unity's bond, our worries cease.
With each gentle breeze, our hearts align,
Forever we fly, on wings so fine.

In every heart, a flame will ignite,
In the dance of the soul, we embrace the light.
Together, we journey, our spirits entwined,
With wings of the Divine, eternally kind.

A Covenant of Strength

In the threads of time, our spirits gather,
Weaving a promise, a bond that matters.
In the silence shared, our hearts convene,
A covenant of strength, sacred and keen.

Through trials faced and burdens borne,
We rise like dawn, in each new morn.
With hands united, we mend the fray,
In the light of love, we find our way.

Each voice a beacon, calling us near,
In the sanctuary of hope, erasing fear.
Through storms of doubt, we find our song,
Bound by the covenant, forever strong.

With every heartbeat, resilience flows,
In the garden of strength, our spirit grows.
Together we stand, in this sacred trust,
In the face of trials, it's love that we must.

For in unity's embrace, we boldly claim,
A covenant of strength, forever the same.
With hearts ablaze, we journey on,
In the book of life, our legacy's drawn.

Armored in Belief

In the shadow of trials, we stand firm,
Our hearts encased, unwavering, true.
Faith, a shield that guards our souls,
Each prayer a sword to cut us through.

With every whisper of doubt that creeps,
We rise, united, in hope's embrace.
Our burdens shared, our spirits bold,
Together we march, hand in hand in grace.

Mountains may tremble, oceans roar,
Yet our armor gleams in the light above.
Trust binds us like a golden thread,
In the tapestry woven by endless love.

In the face of despair, we spread our wings,
Soaring high on faith's gentle breeze.
For those who believe shall never fall,
In the heart of darkness, we find our peace.

From Ashes to Ascension

In the depth of despair, hope is reborn,
Amidst the ashes, a spark ignites.
From shattered dreams we rise anew,
Guided by faith through the stormy nights.

Each step upward, a testament true,
To the strength born of trials endured.
We embrace the fire that shapes our souls,
Forged in the flames, we emerge assured.

The path may be rugged, but we tread on,
With grace as our compass, love as our guide.
Reaching for heaven, we shed our chains,
And in every struggle, our spirits glide.

Rising like phoenixes from the gloom,
We celebrate life, our hearts aflame.
With every ascent, the spirit grows,
In the arms of the Divine, we proclaim.

The journey of faith, a sacred flight,
With each soaring moment, we find our way.
From ashes we rise, eternally bound,
In the light of resurrection, we shall stay.

The Pilgrimage of Strength

Upon the road where many have walked,
Each step taken furthers our quest.
With burdens of sorrow, we carry on,
In search of solace, we seek the blessed.

Through valleys deep and mountains high,
We journey forth, our spirits aligned.
With every stone that scrapes our feet,
We grow resilient, our hearts entwined.

In the whispers of winds, we hear the call,
Inviting us to rise above strife.
Hand in hand with faith as our guide,
We carve a path to a purposeful life.

Moments of doubt may cloud our way,
Yet every tear becomes a prayer.
As we walk this sacred pilgrimage,
The strength of love is always there.

Reaching horizons with fervent hearts,
Together we forge an everlasting bond.
Through life's trials, our courage grows,
In the light of patience, we respond.

Heavenly Fortitude

Through storms and shadows, we find our grace,
A beacon of light in the darkest of night.
With every heartbeat, a song of hope,
Our spirits weave the tapestry bright.

In the quiet moments, strength is revealed,
The whispers of heaven, sweet and near.
With faith as our anchor, we shall not waiver,
United in purpose, we cast out fear.

As clouds may gather, we'll not turn away,
For in every trial, our spirits soar.
With hands lifted high, we embrace the divine,
In the embrace of fortitude, we explore.

Through trials unyielding, we rise and stand,
With hearts intertwined, we gather our might.
For in the embrace of love and belief,
Together we shine, radiant and bright.

So let our voices rise with the dawn,
An anthem of strength, a resonant song.
In the journey of faith, together we tread,
With heavenly fortitude, we'll carry on.

The Hammer of Purpose

With every strike the steel ignites,
A purpose carved in the heart's deep night.
Through trials faced, the spirit's mold,
A testament to faith, strong and bold.

In hands divine, the vision clear,
Each blow resounds, dispelling fear.
Crafted by love, an unveiled art,
The hammer shapes a willing heart.

In labor's toil, the truth is sought,
Lessons learned, and battles fought.
A sacred rhythm, the anvil's song,
Guiding lives where they belong.

With every dent, a lesson learned,
In ember's glow, the soul is burned.
The hammer strikes, the spirit roars,
In destiny's hands, we find our doors.

So let the hammer fall away,
To forge our path, in light of day.
Purpose crafted, strong and free,
In God's great plan, our destiny.

Beneath the Heavens

Under the skies, where stars align,
The whispers of grace in every sign.
Mountains echo with stories old,
In nature's arms, our hearts unfold.

Each dawn breaks soft, a promise new,
The colors dance in vibrant hue.
Mountains bow and rivers flow,
In harmony, creation's glow.

Beneath the heavens, we find our song,
A melody sweet, where souls belong.
Together we stand, hand in hand,
Embracing the love, divinely planned.

The moonlight bathes us in its quilt,
With every dream, our hopes are built.
Clouds may gather, but faith stands tall,
In God's embrace, we won't fall.

So look above, where blessings pour,
Each star a promise, forevermore.
We'll walk this path, with spirits bright,
Beneath the heavens, in His light.

In the Embrace of Adversity

When shadows loom and doubts arise,
In the embrace, our spirit flies.
Through storms we dance, in faith we stand,
A sacred strength, in God's own hand.

The weight we bear, a heavy load,
Yet in our hearts, His love bestowed.
From thorns of life, a rose may bloom,
In trials faced, dispelling gloom.

Each tear that falls, a seed of grace,
In the struggles, we find our place.
For in the fire, we're tried and true,
Emerging pure, as gold anew.

In every challenge, wisdom grows,
Like rivers deep, the spirit flows.
Through darkest nights, the stars still shine,
In adversity's arms, our hearts align.

So let us rise, unbroken souls,
In the embrace, His love consoles.
With every setback, we find our way,
In the trials faced, we learn to pray.

The Balance of Brokenness

In brokenness, the heart finds grace,
A sacred dance, a holy space.
The cracks reveal the light within,
In shattered dreams, new hopes begin.

With every flaw, a lesson learned,
In the ashes, the spirit burned.
From chaos springs a vibrant thread,
In the tapestry, the soul is fed.

The balance holds, both joy and pain,
In every storm, a chance to reign.
For in the struggle, we find our peace,
An understanding, a sweet release.

Though frayed and worn, we wear the scars,
As symbols bright, like ancient stars.
In every wound, a story told,
The balance shines, a truth of old.

So let us dance in broken ways,
In vulnerability, true love sways.
For in the balance, we find the light,
In brokenness, our hearts ignite.

Sanctuary of Courage

In the quiet folds of the night,
Whispers of strength take flight.
Hearts unite in solemn prayer,
Embraced by faith, free from care.

Mountains tremble, yet we stand,
Guided by a steady hand.
For in this sacred, hallowed place,
Courage blooms, wrapped in grace.

Each trial more than mere stone,
In steadfast hearts, we are not alone.
Together we rise through the storm,
In unity, our spirits warm.

With every breath, the promise lives,
Courage thrives as the spirit gives.
In the sanctuary, fear recedes,
For love is the light that leads.

Here we gather, souls aligned,
In the heart of hope, we find.
Courage is our guiding light,
In the sanctuary of the night.

The Scepter of Endurance

Lifted high, the scepter gleams,
In trials faced, we find our dreams.
Through shadows deep, our path is trod,
With every step, we bear the rod.

The weary hearts find solace here,
In whispered truths that draw us near.
Through struggles fierce, we do not yield,
For faith is our unyielding shield.

Each wound a tale of strength imbued,
In every scar, the spirit renewed.
The world may break, but we stand tall,
With endurance, we conquer all.

In the stillness of each dawn's light,
We rise again, our spirits bright.
For every test, a lesson learned,
In the sacred flame, our hearts burned.

Wielding love, we endure the fight,
Guided by the stars at night.
With the scepter, our vision clear,
Endurance sings, our souls sincere.

Light in Dusk

As twilight sways and shadows fall,
A gentle whisper calls us all.
In the dusky hour, hope ignites,
Bathed in grace, our spirits take flight.

Each moment still, a chance to seek,
In silent prayer, the heart may speak.
Through the veil of fading day,
The light of love will guide our way.

With every breath, we find our ground,
In quietude, the truth is found.
Even as the night draws near,
The light within will persevere.

Through tempest winds and darkened skies,
The dawn will break, our spirits rise.
In unity, we cast our doubts,
Embracing light, our faith shouts.

So in the dusky embrace we stand,
Holding tightly to love's command.
For even in darkness, truth we trust,
Guided always by the light of us.

The Weaver's Hands

With gentle touch, the loom does sing,
In threads of hope, love takes wing.
Each knot a tale of joy and pain,
Weaving lives, what grace we gain.

The weaver's hands, so firm yet kind,
In every stitch, the heart aligned.
Patterns forged in trials faced,
In every fabric, love embraced.

Through vibrant hues and shadows grey,
A tapestry of life, we lay.
With every loop, a journey gleams,
The weaver spins the world from dreams.

In the fabric of night, we find,
A sacred place where souls are twined.
For in each thread, a life is sewn,
The weaver's wisdom cherished, grown.

So let us honor, with each strand,
The stories spun by loving hands.
In unity, we rise and stand,
Embraced forever by the weaver's hands.

The Armor of Grace

In shadows deep, where doubts reside,
A cloak of hope is cast aside.
We rise anew, our spirits bold,
With faith, the stories yet untold.

Grace shields us from the fiercest storm,
Guiding our hearts to keep us warm.
In humble hearts, the truth does gleam,
A radiant love, our sacred dream.

With every step, we learn to see,
The light within, our destiny.
Forgiveness blooms where pain has frayed,
In every tear, a prayer relayed.

Let kindness flow like rivers wide,
In unity, we walk beside.
The armor strong, through trials lead,
In every heart, a whispered creed.

And as the dawn breaks through the night,
We're wrapped in grace, a pure delight.
Together we stand, forever blessed,
In love, we find our truest rest.

The Dance of the Unbroken

In the silence, strength is found,
A rhythm rises, soft and profound.
With every heartbeat, we embrace,
The sacred dance of unbroken grace.

The steps may falter; souls may ache,
Yet in this flow, we choose to wake.
Through trials hard and burdens vast,
In faith, we forge our union, cast.

Together we sway, lost in prayer,
Each movement whispers love and care.
Hands united, we lift our voice,
In harmony, we find our choice.

Resilience blooms in every song,
As we embrace where we belong.
The light within, a guiding spark,
Illumines paths through nights so dark.

With every twirl, our spirits soar,
In gratitude, we seek for more.
For in this dance, we find our home,
A world of love where we can roam.

Faithful Resilience

In shadows' grasp, we stand with might,
With every breath, we chase the light.
Through trials faced, we rise anew,
In faith's embrace, our spirits true.

The storms may rage, the winds may howl,
Yet in our hearts, we hear the vowel.
A whispered hope amidst despair,
With faithful steps, we tread with care.

Each challenge met, a lesson learned,
In fiery flames, our souls are burned.
Yet from the ash, we break and rise,
A testament that never dies.

With courage strong, our hearts align,
In unity, the stars will shine.
Bound by love, we forge ahead,
In every word, the promise spread.

And when the path seems hard to tread,
With faithful resolve, we stay ahead.
For in each trial, strength is shown,
In resilience, we are never alone.

Whispers of the Divine Within

In quiet moments, truth awakes,
A gentle pulse, the spirit shakes.
Through stillness deep, we hear the call,
Divine whispers, a love for all.

In every heart, a spark ignites,
Illuminating the darkest nights.
With eyes unclouded, we embrace,
The sacred touch of boundless grace.

The world may try to steal our peace,
Yet from within, our souls release.
With every breath, we seek and find,
The whispers echo, pure and kind.

As seasons turn, we learn to trust,
In trials faced, our faith is just.
For in the silence, louder still,
The divine whispers, shaping will.

So let us nurture, hold so dear,
The sacred voice that calms all fear.
In every heartbeat, love shall grow,
A testament of what we know.

The Bloom of Tenacity

In the garden of trials, we sow,
Faith's gentle whispers, guiding us so.
Through storms of doubt, unwavering stand,
With courage's fire, we hold His hand.

Each petal, a prayer, each thorn, a test,
In the heart's embrace, we find our rest.
Beneath heavy skies, our spirits will rise,
For hope is the sun that lights up the skies.

The roots dig deep where shadows may creep,
In silence we gather the strength that we keep.
With patience, we nurture the seeds of our soul,
And blossom in love, its essence our goal.

In unity, we bloom, a vibrant array,
With faith as our anchor, we conquer the fray.
Together we flourish, through trials we sing,
In harmony's garden, new beginnings we bring.

Let each day unfold, a testament true,
To the bloom of tenacity that lives within you.
In the breath of the Father, our spirits entwined,
Forever we flourish, in love we shall find.

The Eternal Well of Strength

In the depth of our souls, a well does reside,
Where waters of grace flow unceasingly wide.
In moments of sorrow, when courage may fade,
We drink from this source, in His love we're remade.

With each trial we face, the well does not dry,
It fills us with hope, lifts our spirits to fly.
In the silence of prayer, we gather the might,
To face every shadow, to walk in the light.

We dip our hands deep, in the currents of peace,
In the embrace of His mercy, our troubles release.
When burdened with doubt, when weary we tread,
We sip from the well, where our spirits are fed.

In faith's precious cocoon, our hearts become strong,
Resilient and bold, we are never alone.
For the eternal well, no distance can sever,
With each drop we take, we rise anew, ever.

Let the waters of strength pour down from above,
A reminder of grace, an outpouring of love.
In the embrace of the well, we find our way home,
For in His great strength, forever we roam.

In the Eyes of the Faithful

In the eyes of the faithful, a light ever gleams,
Like stars in the heavens, fulfilling our dreams.
With hearts open wide, they gather in prayer,
In the warmth of His promise, they find solace there.

Through trials and tempest, their spirits won't break,
For courage ignites when the path starts to shake.
In every tear shed, there's a story to tell,
Of hope reborn in the depths of a well.

With unwavering trust, they walk side by side,
In the arms of each other, their worries abide.
In the silence of faith, true strength is unveiled,
As echoes of love in their hearts are regaled.

They see through the storm, with vision so clear,
Their eyes don't just look; they see the Divine here.
In the face of despair, their hope will ignite,
For the light of the faithful shines ever so bright.

With each step they take, they carry His grace,
In the eyes of the faithful, love finds its place.
For they are the bearers of truth, pure and bold,
In the stories of faith, their hearts shall be told.

Through the Valley of Shadows

In the valley of shadows, I walk with grace,
The Lord is my guide, in His arms, I find space.
Every step through the darkness, I tread without fear,
For His light is with me, always near.

Mountains may tremble, and storms may roar,
Yet in faith, I stand, trusting evermore.
With each whisper of doubt, I rise to the call,
For the Shepherd beside me will never let fall.

Through trials and tempests, my spirit shall soar,
With the promise of peace, I need nothing more.
In the embrace of His mercy, my heart finds its song,
A melody of hope, where I truly belong.

From shadows I journey, to valleys so wide,
With the strength of His presence, my soul will abide.
No weapon against me shall ever prevail,
For the armor of faith is my unyielding veil.

So I walk through the valley, my head lifted high,
In the light of His love, I shall never die.
With courage as my shield, and truth by my side,
I'll face every shadow with the Savior as guide.

Psalms of the Persevering

Lift thy voice in the still of the night,
For perseverance blooms in the heart's gentle light.
Though the road be long, and the burdens be bare,
In the strength of His presence, we rise from despair.

Let the echoes of sorrow grow faint in the air,
For faith is the anchor, and love is the prayer.
As mountains may crumble, and rivers may bend,
With courage, we press on, to the very end.

In the silence of trials, we find solace true,
For the spirit of hope gently stirs anew.
Each tear that we shed is a seed of grace,
In the garden of trust, we find our place.

Raise your eyes to the heavens, let burdens take flight,
For morning always follows the whispers of night.
With each step we take, may our hearts ever sing,
For the joy of the journey is a glorious thing.

Through the psalms of the persevering, we learn,
With faith as our torch, at each corner, we turn.
Let love be our guide in a world full of strife,
In the promise of glory, we find eternal life.

The Dawn of Resolve

When darkness retreats, and the dawn greets the day,
A resolve in my spirit awakens to stay.
With the sun's gentle rise, my worries release,
For in the light of His grace, I find perfect peace.

Each breath that I take whispers courage anew,
As shadows recede, I embrace what is true.
With heart full of faith, I shall climb every height,
For the dawn of resolve brings strength to my fight.

In the warmth of His promises, I seal my decree,
With every new morning, His love covers me.
Though the world may be tempest, and trials may wane,
In the dawn of His mercy, I rise once again.

Through valleys uncharted and seas that divide,
The dawn of resolve sets my fears aside.
With hope as my compass, I journey ahead,
For the path is made clear, by the light that He shed.

So I welcome the morning, with arms open wide,
In the dawn of resolve, I will ever abide.
With faith as my anchor, in love's sacred realm,
I embrace every challenge, with Him at the helm.

Echoes of the Brave

In the echoes of brave, we find our true voice,
With hearts full of courage, we make our own choice.
Though storms may surround, we stand resolute,
For faith is our armor, and love our pursuit.

Through trials we wander, yet never alone,
In the strength of the faithful, our spirits have grown.
Each step that we take is a testament bold,
To the whispers of hope that are whispered of old.

Let the battles be fought, and the victories sung,
For the echoes of brave in our hearts shall be strung.
With a flame that ignites, we rise with the sun,
In the journey of life, we are never outdone.

So treasure the moments, each heartbeat, each sigh,
For the echoes of brave shall never comply.
With faith as our guide, and love as our friend,
We embrace every challenge, till the very end.

In the chorus of life, let our spirits unite,
In the echoes of brave, we shall walk in the light.
For together we stand, unbroken, and free,
In the harmony forged by His grace, you and me.

The Prayer of Perseverance

In the silence, I seek Your face,
Strengthen my heart, fill this place.
Guide my steps, hold my hand,
With faith unyielding, help me stand.

When trials come, and shadows loom,
Your light, O Lord, shall break the gloom.
With whispered prayers, I rise anew,
In trust, I cling to all that's true.

Through stormy seas, I find my way,
In darkest nights, Your love will stay.
Help me endure, O gracious King,
In every moment, let my soul sing.

The road is long, yet I will tread,
With every tear, I'm gently led.
In perseverance, I find my voice,
In Your embrace, I make my choice.

So let my heart, through pain and strife,
Reflect the power of eternal life.
With prayerful hope, my spirit soars,
In Your embrace, forever yours.

Reflections of Divine Empowerment

In the quiet, Your strength I find,
With every heartbeat, You unwind.
Shackles fall, my spirit takes flight,
In Your presence, I find true light.

You breathe in me a sacred fire,
Lifting my soul, igniting desire.
With every challenge, I rise to claim,
The power within, in Your name.

When weary bones and spirit shake,
Your gentle whispers, I will awake.
Through burdens heavy, I shall move,
With faith unwavering, I will prove.

Let doubts be placed in shadows deep,
With Your assurance, my fears will sleep.
In unity, we face the fight,
Through darkest valleys, You are my light.

So give me courage, Lord divine,
With every struggle, let love shine.
In reflections of Your mighty grace,
I am renewed in Your embrace.

The Gift of Inner Might

A treasure lies within my soul,
A gift of strength that makes me whole.
In moments fraught with pain and doubt,
I find the power to stand and shout.

The storms may rage, the earth may quake,
Yet from my heart, no fear I take.
For You, my Lord, are ever near,
In every struggle, You wipe my tears.

With inner might, I rise each day,
Transform the night into bright day.
In trials faced, I feel the fire,
Your spirit fuels my heart's desire.

No chains that bind me can withstand,
The force of hope, Your guiding hand.
In every challenge, I make my stand,
With faith and love, I understand.

So let my heart be firm and true,
In every step, I walk with You.
The gift of might, a treasure rare,
Forever in Your holy care.

Clouds of Gloom, Rays of Grace

In clouds of gloom, my spirit bends,
Yet deep inside, Your light ascends.
With every shadow, I find my way,
Through darkness, hope will not decay.

Your rays of grace illuminate,
Dispelling fears that hesitate.
In trials vast, Your love will guide,
In peace and strength, I will abide.

Though storms may gather, skies may weep,
In tranquil waters, I find peace deep.
Your gentle whispers dry my tear,
In every struggle, You are near.

With eyes uplifted, I see the dawn,
Through every battle, I'll carry on.
Your endless mercy fills my soul,
In weary moments, You make me whole.

So let my heart in faith applaud,
For every challenge is a gift from God.
In clouds of gloom, with rays so bright,
I walk in confidence, bathed in light.

Threads of Strength

In shadows cast, the light shall rise,
With faith we weave, our hearts in ties.
Each moment's thread, a silent prayer,
In woven bonds, we find our care.

Through trials faced, we stand as one,
In unity, our race is run.
The fabric thick, no tear shall break,
Together strong, we shall not shake.

The tapestry of hope unfolds,
In colors bright, our story told.
With every stitch, we craft our fate,
In love's embrace, we elevate.

So let us hold, each other's hands,
In storms that rage, our spirit stands.
Bound by grace, we rise in song,
In threads of light, we all belong.

Together still, as dawn breaks through,
In every heart, the strength renews.
With every breath, we find the way,
In threads of strength, we choose to stay.

Where Grace Abounds

In quiet walks, where spirits soar,
Where loving hearts seek to restore.
The gentle breeze whispers of peace,
In sacred spaces, worries cease.

Above the clouds, the heavens gleam,
Within our hearts, we dare to dream.
In acts of kindness, grace is found,
In humble love, our souls are crowned.

Through trials fierce, we learn to bend,
In every struggle, grace our friend.
Forgiving hearts, we rise anew,
In every step, His love shines through.

Embracing warmth, we lift our eyes,
In every laugh, a sweet surprise.
Where grace abounds, our spirits sing,
In unity, new hope shall spring.

So let us gather, hand in hand,
In every moment, grace withstands.
In joyful hearts, our lives resound,
In harmony, where grace abounds.

The Call of the Resilient

Amidst the storms, a voice arises,
The call of strength, in heart surprises.
With every trial, our spirit grows,
In paths of light, resilience glows.

Through darkest nights, we navigate,
With faith to guide, we elevate.
In struggles faced, we find our might,
The dawn dispels the veil of night.

In whispered prayers, we find our way,
Together strong, we shall not sway.
The road may wind, yet we press on,
The call of resilient, brightly drawn.

With courage fierce, our hearts ignite,
In every setback, shines the light.
Together striving, hand in hand,
In faith's embrace, we take a stand.

So hear the call, and rise anew,
With every heartbeat, our strength rings true.
In united spirit, choose to thrive,
The call of the resilient keeps us alive.

Fortress of the Heart

In fortress strong, our hearts reside,
With love as shield, we turn the tide.
Against the storms that rage outside,
In faith's embrace, we shall abide.

With every stone, a prayer is laid,
In unity, our fears can fade.
Through trials faced, we build our wall,
In sacred moments, we stand tall.

The light within, a guiding flame,
In darkness deep, we call His name.
In every heartbeat, peace will flow,
In fortress built, our bonds will grow.

So let us guard this sacred place,
With open arms, with boundless grace.
In every challenge, we find our part,
Together strong, a fortress heart.

Through valleys low and mountains high,
In love's embrace, we learn to fly.
In steadfast hearts, our trust we set,
A fortress strong, we won't forget.

The Sculptor's Touch

In silent prayer, hands work with grace,
Forming life from stone, in sacred space.
Each chiselled edge, a life reborn,
In the heart of creation, hope is sworn.

With every strike, a vision is clear,
Divine design, ever drawing near.
Carving dreams from the weight of the past,
In the sculptor's touch, love holds steadfast.

Each fragment speaks, tales of old,
Whispers of faith, in marbles bold.
Transformed in reverence, they rise anew,
In the light of spirit, they break through.

Blessed by the hands, with purpose entwined,
The soul's work unfolds, gentle yet blind.
The sculptor's art, a dance with the divine,
In every creation, the stars align.

As shapes emerge, from dust to light,
Each form a testament, a glorious sight.
Through trials faced, and shadows cast,
In the artist's heart, love holds steadfast.

Garden of Strength

In the garden of life, where blossoms sway,
Faith takes root, and fears drift away.
Nurtured by grace, under watchful skies,
Every petal unfurls, a prayer that replies.

Among thorns and shadows, we learn to grow,
Embracing the storms, the seeds that we sow.
With each rising sun, new hope is born,
In the soil of struggle, resilience is sworn.

The branches of trust stretch wide and tall,
In unity's embrace, we stand through it all.
Blooming with courage, we face the unknown,
In the garden of strength, our spirits have grown.

Raindrops like blessings, watering the earth,
Cleansing the fears, renewing our worth.
Each flower a story, of battles we've fought,
In this sacred space, love has been taught.

With roots intertwined, we will not falter,
Together we rise, as voices alter.
In the garden's embrace, our spirits will sing,
In the light of our faith, we find everything.

The Unyielding Spirit

Through valleys of shadows, the spirit will rise,
Unbroken and bold, beneath endless skies.
With faith as our compass, hearts steady and vast,
The unyielding spirit, forever steadfast.

In trials and storms, we gather our strength,
Finding the path, in struggles' length.
Each challenge we face, a lesson to learn,
In the fires of life, our passions do burn.

No matter the weight, or burden we bear,
Together we stand, in the face of despair.
The spirit unyielding, in darkness we see,
A flicker of hope, a promise to be.

With courage as armor, we march hand in hand,
Embracing the light, like grains of sand.
We soar on the wings of love's gentle song,
The unyielding spirit, forever strong.

So rise up, dear hearts, let your voices be heard,
In unity's strength, we are never deterred.
With the light of the sacred, forever we'll fly,
In the unyielding spirit, we learn to rely.

In Celebration of Struggles

In the tapestry of life, every thread has worth,
Woven together, with purpose and mirth.
Through valleys of sorrow, we find our way,
In celebration of struggles, we merge night and day.

Each challenge a lesson, a chance to evolve,
In the heart of the battle, our fears we dissolve.
With courage we gather, our stories unite,
In the dance of resistance, we shine ever bright.

Every tear a testament, each stumble a song,
In the rhythm of life, we see where we belong.
With faith as our partner, we rise and we stand,
In celebration of struggles, together we've planned.

Through trials and triumphs, we grow ever strong,
Embracing the journey, where we all belong.
Now we sing praises for battles we've fought,
In the celebration of struggles, love is our thought.

So gather, dear spirits, let the stories be told,
In the light of our trials, our hearts turn to gold.
In the celebration of struggles, together we thrive,
In the embrace of our whispers, we come alive.